D0907690

The
Como-Harriet
Streetcar Line

A Memory Trip Through The Twin Cities

TWIN
CITY
LINES

By Aaron Isaacs
and Bill Graham

Copyright © 2002 by the Minnesota Transportation Museum

All rights reserved, including the right to reproduce this work in any form
whatsoever without permission in writing from the publisher,
except for brief passages in connection with a review. For information, write:

The Donning Company Publishers
184 Business Park Drive, Suite 206
Virginia Beach, VA 23462

Steve Mull, General Manager
Rick Taylor, Project Director
Dawn V. Kofroth, Assistant General Manager
Sally C. Davis, Editor
Bridget Belmont, Graphic Designer
John Harrell, Imaging Artist
Scott Rule, Director of Marketing
Gigi Abbott, Marketing Coordinator

Library of Congress Cataloging-in-Publication Data
Isaacs, Aaron, 1949–
    The Como-Harriet streetcar line : a memory trip through the twin cities
      p. cm.
    ISBN 1–57864–168–3 (soft cover : alk. paper)
    1. Street-railroads—Minnesota—Minneapolis Metropolitan Area—History. 2.
Street-railroads—Minnesota—Saint Paul Metropolitan Area—History. 3. Twin City Rapid
Transit Company—History. I. Graham, Bill, 1942–   II. Title.

TF725.M6 I83 2002
388.4'6'09776579—dc21   2002023779

Printed in the United States of America

LEGEND

Chicago	Connecting Lines
■	Point of Interest
··········	Private Right of Way

THE
DONNING COMPANY
PUBLISHERS

Monro

Robbinsdale
N. Washington

2nd St NE

Plymouth

Penn-Fremont

Great
Northern
Depot

6th Ave N

Glenwood

Bryn Mawr

Kenwood

Lake of
the Isles

Nicollet

4th Ave S

St. Louis
Park

31st St

Selby-Lake

Lake
Calhoun

Bryant

HOPKINS

Excelsior Blvd

Hopkins
Trestle

Blake
School

MORNINGSIDE

Lake
Harriet

Lake
Minnetonka

Brookside Loop
1951-54

France

Xerxes

50th St

EDINA

54th St

Penn

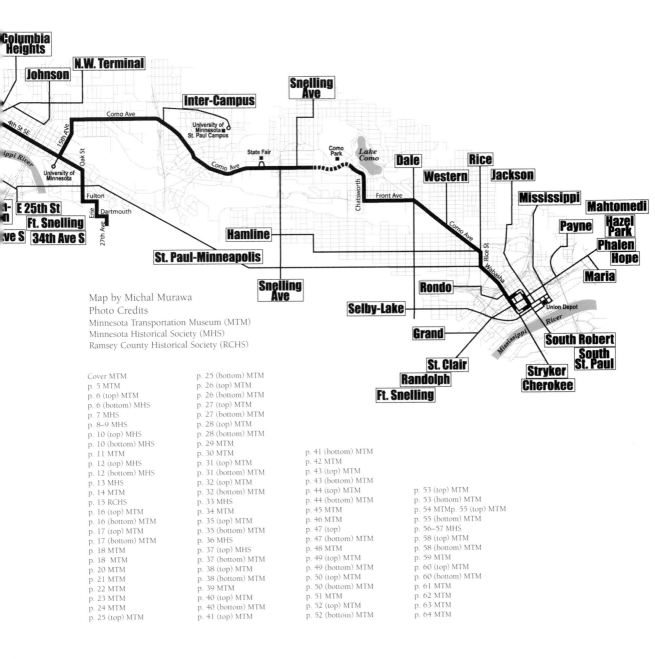

Columbia
Heights

Johnson

N.W. Terminal

Inter-Campus

Snelling
Ave

Como Ave

University of
Minnesota
St. Paul Campus

4th St SE

15th Ave

Oak St

ippi River

University of
Minnesota

Fulton

Erie

Dartmouth

27th Ave

E 25th St

Ft. Snelling

34th Ave S

ve S

Como Ave

State Fair

Como
Park

Lake
Como

Dale

Rice

Western

Jackson

Mississippi

Mahtomedi

Payne

Hazel
Park

Chatsworth

Front Ave

Como Ave

Rice St

Wabasha

Phalen

Hope

Maria

Hamline

St. Paul-Minneapolis

Snelling
Ave

Rondo

Selby-Lake

Union Depot

River

Grand

Mississippi

South Robert

St. Clair

Randolph

Ft. Snelling

Stryker

Cherokee

South
St. Paul

Map by Michal Murawa
Photo Credits
Minnesota Transportation Museum (MTM)
Minnesota Historical Society (MHS)
Ramsey County Historical Society (RCHS)

The
Como-Harriet
Streetcar Line

Looking back, the Como-Harriet line seems to have been the best regarded, most beloved streetcar line in the Twin Cities. It captured the essence of the Twin Cities, the man-made canyons of the downtowns, the tree-lined residential neighborhoods and city parks on private rights-of-way, the shores of beautiful city lakes, the campus of the University of Minnesota, one of the largest state fairgrounds in the United States, and the beautiful State Capitol building-it gave the rider the complete view of both cities without leaving the car. It took passengers down city streets and alleys, over and under narrow bridges, through the woods and across just about every streetcar line in both cities.

Its crowded cars fought city traffic to carry students and workers to and from the busy downtown areas and the University and to the concerts at Lake Harriet.

It is fondly remembered for high speed running on the wooded right-of-way between Lakes Calhoun and Harriet and for the view from the top of the Hopkins trestle.

The Como-Harriet was the second of four Twin City Rapid Transit Company (TCRT) lines linking the two downtowns. Although it wasn't the fastest or busiest line, or the most direct route between the two downtowns, it provided the most enjoyable ride for commuters and sightseers alike. And it was the last streetcar line to be removed from service.

Opposite: Sixth to 7th Street was considered the center of downtown along Hennepin. The block containing the Gopher and Aster Theatres was replaced with City Center.

The route

For most of its service life, the Como-Harriet followed a route that changed little. The Oak-Harriet line shared most of the Minneapolis route with the Como-Harriet. The two split at Dinkytown. Some Oak-Harriet cars terminated their runs at Oak Street SE. next to the University of Minnesota's Memorial Stadium. Others continued past Stadium Village, ending at 27th Avenue Southeast and Yale Avenue. Oak-Harriet cars followed the Como-Harriet route through the private right-of-way past Lakes Calhoun and Harriet, but left it at Xerxes Avenue S. and headed south to 50th Street, then east on 50th to the end of the line at Penn Avenue S. where it met cars from the Bryant-Johnson line.

The steam-powered, narrow-gauge Motor Line first reached Lake Calhoun in 1879. This train to downtown has just departed from the Colonel King's pavilion in the distance.
Below: About 1895, two open cars pass the second Lake Harriet pavilion.

Bustling Hennepin Avenue in the heart of downtown, about 1917. The camera is looking northeast toward 6th Street. The Masonic Temple, Plymouth Building, and Lumber Exchange are still standing.

Between 1906 and 1932, high-speed interurban cars, capable of mile-a-minute speeds, shared the Como-Harriet line but continued west another fifteen miles through Hopkins to the resort communities of Excelsior, Deephaven, and Tonka Bay on Lake Minnetonka. The line was abandoned beyond Hopkins in 1932.

From 1906 until 1951, Como-Hopkins cars shared the Como-Harriet line but continued west on its right-of-way another 4.4 miles to downtown Hopkins just after crossing the famous S-curving Hopkins trestle that bridged a number of railroad tracks.

Throughout most of its busy life, the Como-Harriet began with a counter-clockwise loop around the heart of downtown St. Paul on Wabasha, 5th, Robert, 9th, and Wabasha Streets, the same loop used by the University Avenue line. Climbing away from downtown, the Como-Harriet passed the State Capitol.

Nineteen fourteen saw the opening of the Great Northern Depot at the foot of Hennepin next to the Mississippi River. It replaced the Minneapolis Union Depot, which was across the street.

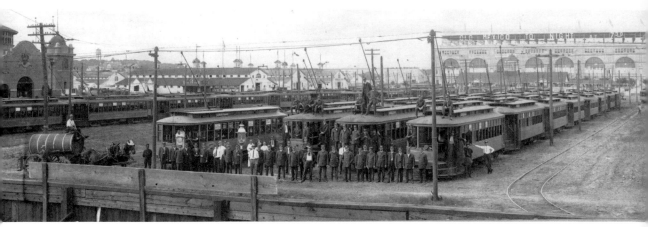

Above: **The Como-Harriet served the State Fair for its entire life. Few people had automobiles in 1912 when this photo was taken, so almost everyone arrived by streetcar. The streetcar yard was located on the north side of Como Avenue, reaching much of the way to the grandstand. Streetcar No. 1267, at far left, survives today at the Seashore Trolley Museum in Maine.**

The line ran north on Rice Street to Como Avenue, west on Como to Front Avenue, north on Chatsworth, then west on private right-of-way through Como Park, passing under the Lexington Parkway bridge that remains to this day.

Below: **This is the main streetcar stop for Como Park. The stone station, always owned by the City of St. Paul, was rebuilt in 2001. The arched footbridge also still exists.**

The cars then left Como Park at Hamline Avenue where they reentered Como Avenue, then across Snelling Avenue and along the southern edge of the Minnesota State Fairgrounds. By design, that meant that all Como-Harriet cars were fairgrounds specials during the ten-day run of the fair each August. At one time a special yard just off Como near Snelling could hold more than one hundred streetcars to handle the state fair passenger traffic.

Como Avenue then became a winding thoroughfare through the planned Victorian community of St. Anthony Park until it reached Eustis Street, the point near the Minneapolis city limits where Minneapolis and St. Paul local cars would wye. This was also the junction where the University of Minnesota's Inter-Campus streetcars left the Como-Harriet line to proceed to the Agricultural Campus in St. Paul.

Three blocks west of Eustis Street is the city limits of Minneapolis. The Como-Harriet cars continued on Como Avenue SE until they turned south on 15th Avenue SE and skirted the northern fringe of the University of Minnesota campus.

The rest of the historic photos in this book follow the Como-Harriet line from downtown St. Paul to Hopkins during the 1930s, 1940s, and 1950s. Passengers are boarding on southbound Wabasha Street at 7th Street, the center of downtown St. Paul.

Above: Como-Harriet and University Avenue cars followed a loop through downtown on Wabasha, 5th Street, Robert Street, and 9th Street. PCC No. 304 is turning from 5th onto Robert. The bottom photo shows the turn from Robert onto 9th Street.

Cars then turned west on 4th Street SE, where they were joined by the Oak-Harriet, and where the Inter-Campus line continued two blocks into the Minneapolis campus. They passed through Dinkytown, proceeded west on 4th Street past large homes that housed students, then crossed Central Avenue and entered the Old St. Anthony area.

Cars turned onto East Hennepin, crossed Nicollet Island past DeLaSalle High School, and then the Mississippi River to the Great Northern Depot. Como-Harriet cars proceeded along Hennepin through downtown, first the Gateway Area, then the bustling theater and commercial district and finally past rows of auto dealerships ending at the Basilica. Past Loring Park, the Plaza Hotel and Walker Art Center and through the infamous (and hair-

The grounds of the State Capitol, viewed from the State Office Building.

raising) Hennepin-Lyndale "bottleneck." After climbing Lowry Hill, named for the streetcar company's longtime president, the cars continued down Hennepin, passing Temple Israel synagogue and West High School. Their last major transfer point was in Uptown at Lake Street, the west terminus of another great interurban line, the Selby-Lake.

The track turned west from Hennepin at 31st Street and headed towards Lake Calhoun. At Irving Avenue, the cars veered south, entering a private right-of-way next to the alley between Irving and James Avenues. The rails were no longer buried in blacktop, concrete, or brick, but completely exposed right down to the wooden ties. The familiar iron bell-top overhead wire poles gave way to wooden poles.

South of 34th Street the view of Lake Calhoun opened up and the fun began. The cars crossed the narrow steel bridge that spanned 36th Street and the motormen turned up the controllers. The speed rose to about 40–45 miles per hour. No more houses. Just open track and woods. Past Lakewood Cemetery and under the William Berry Road to the Lake Harriet Station at 42nd Street, parallel to Queen Avenue, it was a fast ride.

At this intersection, an iron grille fence was placed between the tracks to keep passengers from wandering into the paths of streetcars headed in the opposite direction after they alighted. The large Swiss chalet-style station, with its covered platform, waiting room, and a small grocery store, served passengers and picnickers. Passengers can still board the streetcars of the Minnesota Transportation Museum today at this location.

After leaving 42nd Street the cars continued on the wooded right-of-way as it skirted the northwest shore of Lake Harriet and passed under the Linden Hills Boulevard bridge. Tucked under that bridge today is the Minnesota Transportation Museum streetcar barn, that houses the museum's streetcars and marks the southern end of its line. The right-of-way then curved west to the Linden Hills shopping district at Upton Avenue. From this

Looking east on Como toward Rice Street. The Hamline-Cherokee line is entering Como from Thomas Avenue at right. Bethesda Hospital is in the distance.

Como Park
Station

This aerial photo shows how the streetcar line related to Lake Como. The Como Park station is circled, along with two streetcars on Van Slyke Avenue.

point, the right-of-way again was surrounded by houses and garages and motormen had to crank back on their controllers a bit. Three short blocks later, the Oak-Harriet cars turned south onto Xerxes Avenue.

From Xerxes, the right-of-way got less private as cars had to watch every street crossing until 44th and France. Como-Hopkins cars crossed France and continued on the right-of-way another 4.4 miles to Hopkins until that route was cut back to Brookside Avenue in Edina in 1951. Como-Harriet cars then turned south off of the right-of-way onto France Avenue, the city limits between Minneapolis, Morningside (now part of Edina), and Edina. The cars reached their last commercial district in downtown Edina at 50th Street and proceeded through a residential neighborhood to the end of the line at 54th and France.

No one was heard to say they didn't get their token's worth after a ride on the Como-Harriet line.

The beginning

The Como-Harriet line was created in 1898 by the combination of the Como Avenue and Lake Harriet lines in Minneapolis and the Como Avenue line in St. Paul. But let's go back twenty years and look at how the fragments of what was to be the Como-Harriet were put together.

A westbound PCC carrying Como-Hopkins signs emerges from under Lexington Avenue, just west of the Como Park station. The bridge still carries traffic.

Looking west from the Lexington Avenue Bridge, the streetcar passes through the middle of Como Park.

The earliest traces of the line began in June 1878 when the Minneapolis Street Railway (MSR) granted a lease to the newly formed Lyndale Railway Company to build a line powered by steam motors (the public even referred to it as The Motor Line) from downtown Minneapolis to the then city limits at 26th Street. In 1879, the company built a narrow-gauge (3 feet between the rails) 4.5-mile single-track line out 1st Avenue South (now Marquette Avenue) and Nicollet Avenue to 31st Street, then west to Lake Calhoun, ending at 34th Street.

In 1880, the company extended the single-track on private right-of-way from Lake Calhoun to Lake Harriet. The company changed its name to Minneapolis, Lyndale & Minnetonka Railway in 1881 to reflect its new line extension from Lake Harriet to Excelsior, a distance of fifteen miles. On June

Looking both ways at Hamline Avenue. Westbound cars left the private right-of-way at this point, entering tree-lined Como Avenue.

17

This is Como and Snelling, beginning of the State Fair grounds. The curving track at left is the Snelling Avenue line, which used the Como rails between Snelling and Pascal.

15, 1882, the first train reached the resort community of Excelsior on the shores of Lake Minnetonka. However, success of the extension was short-lived and, due to financial problems, the track from Lake Harriet to Excelsior was abandoned in 1886 and service was temporarily cut back to Lake Calhoun. But the right-of way between Lakes Calhoun and Harriet didn't remain dormant for long.

In 1887, the MSR leased The Motor Line, restored service to Lake Harriet, and constructed a pavilion on the northwest shore of the lake, later building a waiting station/platform at 42nd Street. The line was operated with steam equipment until August 19, 1890.

Electric streetcars had become practical in 1887, and companies across the country soon converted to the new power source. On September 22, 1890, a new electric line opened, replacing the steam motor operation from downtown Minneapolis to 31st Street. By May 24, 1891, the electric line was complete out to Lake Harriet. At the same time, the track gauge was widened to standard gauge (4 feet-8.5 inches between the rails). To further call attention to this great improvement, the right-of-way from Lake Calhoun to Lake Harriet was illuminated at night by forty powerful arc lights attached to overhead poles as an attraction.

The same year, MSR constructed a second Lake Harriet pavilion to replace the 1887 building that had burned down. Track changes were made on August 13, 1891, that rerouted the Lake Harriet line out Hennepin Avenue instead of Nicollet Avenue from downtown Minneapolis to 31st Street, the route it would follow the rest of its life.

Como meets Harriet

Streetcar service to the State Fair ended in 1953.

The second streetcar line between the downtowns was created when tracks on Como Avenue in Minneapolis and St. Paul were joined at the city limits on July 1, 1898, creating the Como Interurban or Como-Interurban-Harriet streetcar line. At the same time, TCRT began building its own distinctive style of double-truck cars at its shops at 31st and Nicollet. The first twenty cars manufactured were placed on the new Como-Interurban-Harriet line.

A siding on the Lake Harriet right-of-way between Upton and Xerxes was built and used for storing extra cars to meet the 10 p.m. evening traffic rush generated by the band concerts, pleasure boating, and swimming at Lake Harriet. The siding was double-ended, but during the winter months, the switch at the west end was removed.

In 1905, the Como-Harriet was extended again to Hopkins and Lake Minnetonka, reaching the lake at Excelsior, Deephaven, and Tonka Bay. There the streetcars transferred passengers to company built steamboats that traveled to all points on the lake.

Just west of the fairgrounds, Como makes a sweeping curve. This looks west from Knapp Avenue.

The final years

The first line to abandon the Lake Harriet right-of-way was Lake Minnetonka, cut back to 9th Avenue in downtown Hopkins in 1932. In August 1951, the Como-Hopkins line was abandoned, but a portion of the right-of-way through Edina was kept intact. A loop was installed on the east side of the Minneapolis, Northfield & Southern Railroad bridge near Brookside Avenue. Finally in the wee hours of June 19, 1954, on schedule, the Como-Harriet line came to an abrupt end when the last car pulled into East Side Station at 1:34 a.m., loaded with rail fans who bid the old line farewell.

Remembering the Como-Harriet

—Bill Graham
Summer of 1947

In the summer of 1947, the southwestern neighborhoods of Minneapolis were a comfortable mix of older houses with attics and front porches on streets lined with big elm trees. People sat on their front porches to eat their meals, visit with their neighbors and sleep away stifling summer nights. Air-conditioning could be found in movie theaters and passenger trains of the time, but when the summer was hot, people were hot.

In 1947, small children looking for excitement could count automobiles passing their homes, sometimes as many as twenty in a half-hour on busier streets. Grandparents could be counted on to lead the way to Lake Harriet to

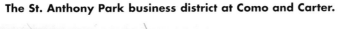

The St. Anthony Park business district at Como and Carter.

Looking toward Minneapolis on Como just west of Eustis Street. That's the Minnesota Transfer Railroad bridge. Highway 280 has not yet been built.

angle for tiny bluegills and perch. Each spring, neighborhood streets were a mass of potholes from the winter's frost, and city public works crews driving Caterpiller tractors provided the highlight entertainment. In the morning, they would plow up a street as one would a vegetable garden. In the afternoon, they graded the street level and squirted fragrant asphalt oil over it. Finally, a roller would compress the whole works into something like flatness. After a week of excitement, the machinery disappeared for another year.

Along Xerxes Avenue in 1947, pile drivers banged in the footings for new expansion bungalows. The tracks of the Oak-Harriet streetcar line, like the tracks on France Avenue, were laid in an oiled earth roadway where railheads stuck up above the surface to jerk automobiles off course and bring harsh words from parents and grandparents alike about the terrible condition of the street. That summer, "The Streetcar Company," as people called it, took big corrective action. First one track, then the other was re-laid with new ties and rails in a concrete bed. Then a new all-concrete roadway was poured over the tracks so that automobile tires could cross back and forth over the railhead without so much as a twitch.

Children and their grandfathers daily watched this performance unfold. Work streetcars, some painted dark red, others yellow and green, plied back and forth. Some had big cranes mounted on them while others unloaded sand and gravel or rails and ties. Some carried tools for welders to fasten the new rail sections together using pots that belched fire and smoke. It was great entertainment. Best of all, both streetcars and automobiles now could run smoother and faster on the avenue, and everyone agreed it was progress.

In a couple of years, new streetcars appeared on Xerxes Avenue. Streamlined, quiet and softly sprung, they could dance a jig while waiting at a stop light, then tear off leaving the automobiles behind when the light turned green. Inside, they were crisp and fresh with rubber floors, padded seats and exotic, dark green windows for standing passengers. Best of all, they were so quick and quiet that a person could hardly hear them approach if he or she were not watching. With their new white on black destination signs and bright lights, they proved again that life in Minneapolis truly was getting better and better.

Riding Downtown

The best place to ride on the Oak-Harriet streetcar was the first peanut row seat on the left side. Here, one could watch the motorman handle the

A Como Avenue institution is Manning's at 22nd Avenue, next to the Northern Pacific Railroad overpass.

Boarding passengers on Wabasha at 7th Street in the heart of downtown St. Paul. This particular car is headed for South St. Paul, sharing the same tracks in downtown as the Como-Harriet.

controls, view the track ahead and see who climbed aboard. Riding downtown felt like one of those radio shows of the period that started with a tour of the neighborhood. One passed the same homes along Xerxes Avenue and recalled where an acquaintance lived or wondered again who might live in the especially interesting house. As on "Allen's Alley" or "The Great Gildersleeve," familiar people boarded the car each time one rode it, people with a distinctive face or manner, women who wore unusual hats, who smelled or spoke in a particular way, and people who always sat in the same seat. Friendly people and crabby people; people who looked crabby but might not have been; and people whose children did not behave as well as they should when traveling downtown on the streetcar. It was all right to speak to strangers so long as one spoke politely in a low voice.

Turning onto the private right of way between 44th and 43rd Streets, the sound changed as the wheels squealed then sang along the open track, the weeds dancing to the car's whoosh. Like a whistle stop in a small town, the car braked between the commercial buildings to stop at busy Upton Avenue, where the 39th Street shuttle bus waited to exchange passengers. This was Linden Hills, where getting off meant visiting the Library, Stillman's Grocery, Clark Hardware, or the Five and Dime where penny candies were sold from

The sumac is turning red in September 1951 as an eastbound car parallels 44th Street through Edina.
Below: A St. Paul-bound car turns from Rice Street onto Wabasha, just west of the State Capitol.

A Minneapolis-bound car approaches Eustis Street, near the city limits, where the Inter-Campus line from the Agricultural Campus joined the Como-Harriet. Luther Theological Seminary sits on the hill in the distance.
Below: The S & L Department Store and the old Labor Temple sat on 4th Street Southeast at Central Avenue.

The Great Northern Depot on Hennepin Avenue at the river.
Below: **Southbound on Hennepin Avenue at 28th Street.**

A PCC car stops at the Lake Harriet station.
Below: Looking west from Chowan Avenue towards France Avenue and the
Minneapolis city limits.

small, open trays and carried off in tiny brown bags. The lady in the children's book section at the Linden Hills Library always greeted visitors warmly even though she could not remember their names. The hardware store man whom all the adults knew talked about paint, putty, and screen doors. It was always the same: fun, familiar, and reassuring.

The track ran downhill from Upton Avenue toward Lake Harriet, first passing the abandoned loop track just east of the dimestore, then turning sharply to duck under Linden Hills Boulevard where cars rarely stopped. Anticipation built for the fast ride that was coming, and for that elevator ride up to the 10th or 12th floor of the Medical Arts Building. A visit to Dayton's Department Store would be fun where a miniature train carried Santa's visitors around the auditorium floor at holiday time.

Lake Harriet Station seemed like a real small town depot with its roofed platform where the lights burned day and night, and where in its waiting

An Oak-Harriet car approaches the end of the line at 50th and Penn Avenue.

Turning onto Como from 15th Avenue Southeast.

room, one could stock up on hotdog buns, ketchup, and pickles for picnics in the Glen. Also at Lake Harriet Station, one could buy small fruit pies in paper wrappers for munching at band concerts. Even elderly folks noted that orchestras had played at Lake Harriet bandstand each summer for as long as anyone could remember. Afterwards, concertgoers crowded the station platform waiting for streetcars headed downtown or back home to southwest Minneapolis, Edina, and Hopkins.

At family picnics in the Lake Harriet Glen, the hot dogs, jungle gyms, and family had to compete for attention with the rush hour streetcar action just a few yards away. As streetcars charged past every few minutes, boys looked for creative ways to get involved in the drama. The wire fence, meant to keep them off the track, didn't. A roll of paper caps, left over from the Fourth of July, would make a deafening report when run over by the steel wheels. Dads inquired, of course, and the boys denied all knowledge, of course.

Even better were the blue flames that a trolley wheel made if one could pour water on it at just the right moment. By standing on Berry Bridge at twilight and saving up a large amount of saliva, boys and their brothers could make fireworks by letting fly just when the trolley passed beneath them. With the scents of hot dogs and wood smoke in the air, the Lake Harriet

After leaving Dinkytown, 15th Avenue passes under the Great Northern Railway.

Below: This is the end of the line for some of the Oak-Harriet cars. To turn around, cars backed into the wye track on Beacon, a block north of Oak and Washington. Others continued to 27th and Yale SE. Looming over everything is the University of Minnesota's Memorial Stadium.

A Como-Harriet car turns from 15th Avenue onto 4th Street, joining the Oak-Harriet tracks that enter from the right side of the photo. The Inter-Campus line continued straight ahead on 15th. The entire intersection was, and still is, located on a bridge over yet another railroad corridor.

Below: Boarding passengers on 4th Street at 14th Avenue, the center of Dinkytown.

Looking down 4th Street Southeast toward Dinkytown from 10th Avenue.

Glen would have been just another picnic area without the Como-Harriet streetcars.

Until now, motormen had kept opening and closing their controllers in order to hold down their speed for frequent stops and auto traffic. Now, looking down a mile of track on private right-of-way, and with the controller shoved all the way into the left hand corner, the streetcar rocketed past the picnic glen, under Berry Road bridge, and down the straightaway beside Lakewood Cemetery. With fragrant summer wind whipping through open windows and wheels singing on silky smooth rail, this was the thrill ride to end all. Swooping over the viaduct above 36th Street, the car snaked above the bluff at Lake Calhoun before tiptoeing down the three blocks of alleyway to 31st Street. Here, one saw garages and vegetable gardens pushed up against the fence and laundry drying on the line.

Lake Street and Hennepin Avenue, major transfer point with the Selby-Lake crosstown cars, was where one shopped at Morris & Christie's or Hove's grocery stores, ate lunch at the Hasty-Tasty, and stocked up on one-cent bottles of Rexall aspirin which grandparents took for their rheumatism. Matinee movies at the Uptown or Granada Theaters featured newsreels and cartoons, followed by cowboy action thrillers and sentimental stories about dogs and horses.

All the way down Hennepin Avenue, the rider could watch the progress of the streetcar reflected in the windows of the shops. As the car appeared to rise and fall according to the angle of each store window, the seats filled up and people stood in the aisle. Rounding the curve north of Franklin Avenue and descending Lowry Hill, the rails of the Bryant Avenue car line merged by the Hennepin Avenue Methodist Church. Autos, buses, and streetcars came and went in all directions. As Loring Park and the Basilica passed, people got up to head for the doors. Hennepin Avenue always was alive with people on foot visiting the shops, restaurants, and theaters, or transferring to another car line. At the foot of Hennepin Avenue, the cars stopped at the front door of the Great Northern Depot where people with suitcases caught trains to places only dimly imaginable. This was downtown where important people did big things and met in important places.

Returning home by evening streetcar was a more serious experience. Peering down Hennepin Avenue, one saw six, eight, or ten streetcars lined up, their dim yellow ceiling lights barely illuminating the destination signs. "Como-Harriet to 54th." "Oak-Xerxes." "Como-Harriet." "Oak-Harriet."

Turning from 4th Street onto East Hennepin, joining the Bryant-Johnson and North West Terminal lines.

East Hennepin used to be lined with businesses where it crossed Nicollet Island. This westbound car is crossing the Mississippi River past the landmark Grain Belt Beer sign.

This is Bridge Square, where Nicollet Avenue used to meet Hennepin. The park at left was called the Gateway, and its name extended to the surrounding skid row district. The Nicollet Hotel looms in the distance.

"Lyndale & Lake." "Como-Hopkins." "Como-Harriet to 50th." "Bryant to 56th." "Bryant to 54th & Penn." One after another, they eased past the corner with standing loads. No schedules. If one missed his or her car, another would be along in a few minutes. Autos had to stop at the yellow "Safety Zone" signs to let passengers cross from the curb to board their cars.

In winter, windows steamed up and the cars smelled of warm, wet wool. Men stood on the rear platform where smoking was permitted but not children. In heavy snow, autos struggled with ice or simply fell in behind the streetcar, their tires matching the width of the rails. Waiting for one's car in the evening at one of the stops along the private right-of-way, an endless line of yellow headlights stretched for blocks as loaded cars whizzed past. The

Southbound passengers board in the middle of downtown, at 7th and Hennepin. Not surprisingly, a crowd of people in the street didn't mix well with automobiles. The City tried to minimize this problem by painting an area for boarding passengers on the pavement, and installing "Safety Zone" signs, like the one shown here.

Above: Hennepin at 8th Street, transfer point to the Chicago-Penn-Fremont line. Metro Community College now occupies the Northwestern Bank Lincoln office building and the Pantages Theater has been restored.

Below: Looking south from 9th Street at the Orpheum Theater and, at far left, the old Minneapolis downtown library.

From 12th Street to the Basilica, Hennepin was lined with auto dealers and related businesses.

At the intersection of Wayzata Boulevard (note Highway 12 sign). Hennepin turned southwest, passing the Basilica.

order of the evening was to keep them all moving and get folks home. People said "good night" to each other as they clumped down the rear steps to the street where automobiles waited patiently for them to cross.

The Como-Harriet streetcar line was a neighborhood necessity and a safe, but alluring way for the young rider to join the adult world of the city, sharing in its sense of urgency and moment. The yellow streetcars, the people who ran them and rode them day and night, in good weather and bad, year after year, showed what a serious and fascinating business it was to live and work in the city.

The yellow streetcars disappeared just as the first baby boomers entered their teens and moved to the suburbs. New neighborhoods, new friends, and a whole new lifestyle based around the automobile, quickly became familiar reality, even as the streetcars and the city they served just as quickly receded into memory. But their absence left a hole in the fabric of the city and in people's lives. No longer could a young explorer walk to the corner and for eleven cents roam the city with total confidence, innocent of schedules, and free to satisfy his or her curiosities. And the Lake Harriet Glen was silent on summer evenings.

The huge intersection of Hennepin and Lyndale Avenues in front of the Walker Art Center was called the "Bottleneck," and traffic crossed it without benefit of traffic signals. The camera is looking north from the Thomas Lowry statue. The Como-Harriet line followed Hennepin, at left, while Bryant-Johnson cars swung onto Lyndale Avenue at right.

Turning 180 degrees from the previous photo, this view looks south on Hennepin as it climbs Lowry Hill. Thomas Lowry, builder of the streetcar system, built his mansion on the west side of Hennepin next to the Walker Art Center. His statue, at left, now sits at 24th and Hennepin.

Images of the Como-Harriet
—John Diers

In the summer of 1950 my parents and I took an apartment in the Meadowbrook Manor complex on Excelsior Blvd. in St. Louis Park, near today's Methodist Hospital. As I entered the second grade, I was nuts about

This southbound car is at Franklin Avenue. Becky's Cafeteria, a longtime Lowry Hill institution, is at far left.

40

streetcars and trains. My dad invested heavily in an American Flyer layout and often took me downtown to watch the trains come and go at the Great Northern and Milwaukee depots. On Saturdays, the great treat was the streetcar ride with my grandparents. We eventually rode most of the car lines in the Twin Cities, but our trips always began on the Como-Hopkins line.

Facing the other way (south) at Franklin. This scene has changed very little since then. *Below:* **Looking south at the intersection of Hennepin and Fremont, just south of 25th Street.**

One could ride the Glen Lake–Excelsior bus to downtown from Meadowbrook Manor, but I protested mightily that I didn't like buses. The dark green Macks on the Excelsior line were noisy, smelly, and rough riding. It was hard to believe my parents who said they were planning to replace the streetcars with these things. Why would they do something like that? My grandparents sympathized, and so we'd drive into Hopkins on Saturdays to catch the Como-Hopkins car at the end of the line and spend the whole day riding the streetcar system.

A northbound car crosses 28th Street. West High School is at right.

For a seven-year-old, who barely could climb the steps, the big yellow cars were awesome. Once aboard and perched on the peanut row seat just behind the motorman, I could watch him work the controller and air brakes. Our Saturday trips became regular enough that one motormen got to know my grandparents and me. During his layover in Hopkins, he let me sit on the motorman's seat and explained in detail the various controls and switches. At departure time, with the steady bing-a-bing-a-bing of the air compressor and a whoosh of releasing brakes, we began the run to downtown Minneapolis.

Our car crawled out of the wye, paused briefly at Excelsior Boulevard and drifted down the Ninth Avenue single track until we reached the long, tall

Entering Uptown. The streetcar is at Lagoon Avenue, which at the time did not extend east of Hennepin.

Below: Lake and Hennepin, with the Uptown Theater and the Rainbow Cafe. The Selby-Lake line tracks diverge at right.

viaduct over the tracks of the Milwaukee Road, Great Northern and Minneapolis & St. Louis railways. We crossed the viaduct slowly for good reason: the track was far, far above the ground. On the other side, however, we crossed Highway 18 (Washington Avenue) and speed picked up. Some motormen notched out their controllers slowly and carefully, while others threw them into the left-hand corner. Sometimes the car paused or shuddered before it picked up speed as the traction motors dug in.

The line ran on private right of way all the way to 31st and Irving Avenue in south Minneapolis. In 1950 the area between Hopkins and Brookside Avenue was undeveloped, open country and marshland. Except for the rare

Turning from 31st Street onto Hennepin, passing the Morris & Christie Market.
Below: **Private right-of-way began at 31st and Irving, and that's why the building at left, still standing, is shaped the way it is.**

pause at Blake Road, we usually ran all the way to Morningside before stopping to pick up a passenger. It was a wonderful ride, especially on a warm day with all the windows open. Although it seemed much faster, the car might have hit 40 MPH, since the track was rough. Had I been older, I might have figured out that the rough track and dearth of passengers presaged the line's abandonment west of Brookside Avenue within the year, and that the whole system would be gone four summers later.

Abandonment seemed unimaginable as we banged over the special work at France Avenue and stopped across from the weedy 44th Street loop to pick up a few passengers. In 1952 a paving project forced abandonment of the track on France Avenue, and thereafter, Como-Harriet cars turned back at 44th Street just east of France Avenue. At Hennepin Avenue and Lake Street

Streetcar No. 1300, now owned by the Minnesota Transportation Museum, unloads a passenger at 33rd Street, as it parallels the alley between Irving and James Avenues.

45

South of 34th Street, the right-of-way left the alley and swung closer to Lake Calhoun, visible through the trees at right. This is now a walking path.

we encountered buses on the Nicollet-Hennepin and the Excelsior-Glen Lake lines. I pointed to them complaining how they smelled and blocked our progress. As we passed Lagoon Avenue, I noted the granite pavers, which marked the path of the St. Louis Park car line, abandoned in 1938. I couldn't believe that the same fate awaited the Como-Harriet. At Douglas Avenue there were more pavers, sans track, marking the fate of the Kenwood Line, which also disappeared before WWII. Finally, at Lyndale Avenue the Bryant-Johnson line joined up alongside Tom Lowry's statue and PCC cars appeared. Once downtown, we'd transfer to another Minneapolis line, or more likely, stay on the Como-Hopkins and ride through to downtown St. Paul, have lunch at Lee's Broiler, ride a couple of the St. Paul lines out and back, and return via the Selby-Lake.

Our Saturday streetcar rides continued for two years. We covered almost every remaining line in the Twin City Rapid Transit Company system. We even got an impromptu tour of the Snelling Avenue carhouse in St. Paul thanks to an old friend of my Grandfather's who worked for TCRT.

The tracks crossed 36th Street on a bridge. The camera is looking down the hill toward Lake Calhoun.

Below: This is the Cottage City stop under the William Berry Road Bridge, where the museum streetcars now operate.

My parents bought a home in suburban Bloomington far away from the Como-Harriet streetcar line. As my interests shifted to science, chemistry sets and microscopes displaced my trains. The American Flyer layout gathered dust, and my father put it away in barrels. I took up amateur radio and was studying for my ham radio license. In June 1954, my grandfather sent me a newspaper clipping announcing that the streetcars were gone for good. I barely noticed and didn't lament their passage. I stuck the clipping in a book and forgot about it.

Along the way, I rekindled my old interests, went to college, and made my career in public transit systems. I even learned to like buses and PCC streetcars. More recently, I came across one of my old books on Ham Radio. There, stuck in the middle, was a yellowed newspaper clipping and a note from my Grandfather lamenting the passage of the streetcars. All the memories came back.

The Lake Harriet Glen, with Lake Harriet in the distance and houses fronting Queen Avenue at right.

The Lake Harriet station at 42nd Street, viewed from the north. Queen Avenue is at right. Passengers headed for the lake got off at the platform in the foreground and passed under the tracks via the pedestrian subway.

Below: The Swiss chalet depot, designed by architect Harry Wild Jones and built in 1914. It housed a small store and a holding cell where the park police could detain the occasional ruffian.

Climbing away from Lake Harriet, this car is about to pass under Linden Hills Boulevard.

Below: There was a station at Linden Hills Boulevard, and the west steps remain today. The track in the foreground is now a public alley.

Excuse the light flare at left, but unpublished views of the streetcar crossing Upton Avenue are rare.

THE MINNESOTA TRANSPORTATION MUSEUM

The Minnesota Transportation Museum was formed to save a single streetcar, Twin City Lines No. 1300. Typical of the 1,140 wood standard cars designed and built in the company's own shops, No. 1300 was one of only two that survived the 1954 TCRT abandonment completely intact. Donated to the Minnesota Railfans Association, a group that specialized in rail fan trips during the '40s, '50s and '60s, it was moved to a rail siding in Hopkins and there it sat for eight years, weathering under a tarp.

MTM was incorporated in 1962, and No. 1300 was moved to the Minnesota Transfer Railway's roundhouse in St. Paul. A new roof was fabricated and all the bad wood in the carbody replaced. A generator was rigged up on a handcar to supply electricity and in May 1963, it ran under its own power.

MTM was left with the question, "What now?" The car was done, but it had no place to operate. Undeterred, MTM announced that No. 1300 would operate back and forth in the transfer's railyard for the public. Despite the completely unglamorous setting, ten thousand people showed up over several days. The waiting line was a city block long at times, and the MTMers realized that the public would support an operating museum.

Looking west from Upton Avenue. The windowless building is an electrical substation for the streetcars. Just beyond it and behind St. Thomas Church, was a third track where extra cars were staged to return the Lake Harriet crowds to the city. The right-of-way became parking for local businesses, including Great Harvest Bakery at left and Bayer's Hardware at right.

Below: The Oak-Harriet line diverged at right onto Xerxes Avenue.

Looking north on Xerxes from 44th Street at an Oak-Harriet car turning off the right-of-way.

Below: **Looking north from the intersection of 49th and Xerxes.**

But where to operate? The best known and most scenic part of the Twin City Lines system had been the high speed private right-of-way to Lake Harriet in southwest Minneapolis. Upon abandonment in 1954, the Minneapolis Park Board had assumed ownership, and much of the grade lay untouched. MTM negotiated a lease. A simple metal carbarn was erected under the Linden Hills Boulevard bridge, in order to be as unobtrusive as possible. The first block-and-a-half of track was laid as far as the old Lake Harriet station at 42nd Street. Part of the original concrete platform was all that remained of the Swiss Chalet-style building. Operations began in 1971 sans overhead wire, using the noisy but reliable gasoline generator.

Turning from westbound 50th onto Xerxes. This intersection was the end of the line for some cars, signed Oak-Xerxes, and they pulled straight ahead onto the wye track at lower right.

Overhead was strung in 1973. Gradually the line grew, reaching its present terminus at Lake Calhoun in 1977. With No. 1300 running daily all summer long, there was clearly a need for a second car to share the load. Twin City Lines had sold dozens of carbodies for use as sheds or other structures. Members had made a small industry out of locating them and stripping any usable parts as a hedge against the future.

The wye on Penn Avenue just north of 50th Street, shared with Bryant-Johnson cars. The wye is the reason that Penn is wider for a short distance north of 50th.

One of these forays into the north woods uncovered an expected treasure, Duluth streetcar No. 265. Twin City Lines had managed the Duluth system and built most of its cars to standard TCRT designs at Snelling shops. No. 265 was actually built as TCRT No. 1791 in 1915, and was sold to Duluth in 1916. It ran there until the system was abandoned in 1939. The body was

Between Abbott and France Avenues, the right-of-way ran along the north side of 44th Street. This view looks east and downhill from the 44th and France loop. The loop switches are visible before the oncoming streetcar and at far right.

Fiftieth and France was considered the downtown of Edina for many years. The Edina Theater is at right. The short line wye track is in the foreground.

then used as a cabin at Solon Springs, Wisconsin, where it was preserved in sound condition. In 1973, the car was transported to MTM's restoration shop. No. 265 was disassembled and the wood and metal parts were reconditioned or replaced. The classic problem of no wheels, motors, and electrical gear was solved by what model railroaders would call kit bashing. The museum acquired two trailer trucks from Chicago Transit Authority L cars and motors came from an electric locomotive that once served at TCRT's St. Anthony Falls steam power plant in Minneapolis. It entered service in 1982.

The restoration crew next tackled an even more ambitious project, Duluth streetcar No. 78, built in 1893. A small car typical of its era, all that was left was the shell of a body. Many felt the project was hopeless, but the original frame and interior woodwork was saved in the restoration. New electrical and air brake systems were created, and an authentic Brill-

Almost at the 54th Street end of the line, passing houses on France at about 52nd Street. *Below:* An eastbound car has just left the stop at Wooddale Avenue. The tracks are paralleling 44th Street.

In 1951, the line was cut back from Hopkins to this loop just east of Brookside Avenue. This picture is framed by the Minneapolis, Northfield & Southern railroad trestle. Highway 100 crosses in the distance.

designed motor truck was obtained from Brussels, Belgium. After five years of diligent rebuilding, No. 78 made its maiden run in 1990.

TCRT was unique in never owning a steel-bodied streetcar until the first modern PCC car arrived in 1946. The PCC was a design created in the 1930s in a last effort to build something modern and attractive enough to compete with the automobile. By 1949 there were 141 PCC's on the property, but all were sold in 1953, as new management prepared to convert the transit system to buses. They went to Newark, Shaker Heights, Ohio, and Mexico City, and proved to be a durable group. The Newark cars remained in service until 2001, although two of these were sold to Shaker Heights (Cleveland) in 1978. In 1991, the museum, with assistance from the Metropolitan Transit Commission, purchased the pair from the Cleveland transit agency. The better of the two, No. 322, underwent a complete rebuilding, and entered service in 2000.

In 1990 a replica of the 1900 Linden Hills depot was built on its original site. For the first time, the reborn streetcar line had a place to sell tickets and souvenirs, and to house interpretive displays.

Another view of the Brookside loop, looking southeast from the railroad bridge over 44th Street. The water is Minnehaha Creek.
Below: The stop at Blake School.

Museum line follows original line closely

Minnesota Transportation Museum's restored Como-Harriet Streetcar Line is an authentic recreation of a portion of the original line. Most of the route follows the right-of-way laid out by the Motor Line in 1880. The single-track narrow-gauge line gave way to a double-track standard gauge line with the introduction of electric cars in 1891. The line then remained unchanged

There was still plenty of open land between Minneapolis and Hopkins in 1950. This is looking east from the Hopkins trestle towards Washington Avenue, now Highway 169.

until abandonment of the street railway system in 1954. TCRT quickly removed the rails for salvage, but left the ties.

When MTM relaid the rails in 1970 and 1971, members spiked down the museum's single track directly on TCRT's old southbound trackbed from the Linden Hills bridge to the pedestrian overpass just north of 42nd Street. The concrete overpass still had the old rail anchors so alignment at that point was

61

fairly accurate. The passing siding at 42nd Street was laid on TCRT's old northbound mainline from 42nd Street, north across the overpass, and about two hundred feet down the wooded right-of-way.

North of that point, the single track was laid in the middle of the old double track right-of-way since the museum does not plan to lay a second mainline track. The track goes under the center of the William Berry Bridge. Here, the route's identical match to the original line ends.

TCRT cars used to sail on past the William Berry Bridge fairly straight to the 36th Street bridge about four blocks away, which explains why they were able to reach such high speeds through the area. After 1954, Lakewood Cemetery annexed all of the TCRT right-of-way adjacent to its property from the William Berry Bridge north to 36th Street. The MTM track had to be laid on a new alignment through this section alongside the cemetery.

In 1954, the old 36th Street streetcar bridge was dismantled, the stone block abutments removed, and the banks graded back into gentle slopes on both sides of 36th Street. Between 34th and 36th Streets, the old grade has been turned into a footpath. The 35th Street station is still in place.

The highlight of any ride to Hopkins was this S-curving trestle that climbed over a series of railroad tracks.

After leaving the trestle, Hopkins-bound cars followed this curve onto 9th Avenue, past the offices of Minneapolis-Moline, manufacturer of farm equipment.

On summer afternoons and evenings since 1971, new generations have been able to experience the sight, sound and feel of the trolley on the Minnesota Transportation Museum's restored Como-Harriet Streetcar Line.